Wilson Reading System®

Student Reader Four

THIRD EDITION

by Barbara A. Wilson

Wilson Language Training Corporation

www.wilsonlanguage.com

Wilson Reading System® Student Reader Four

Item # SR4AB

ISBN 1-56778-070-9

THIRD EDITION (revised 2004)

The Wilson Reading System is published by:

Wilson Language Training Corporation
175 West Main Street
Millbury, MA 01527
United States of America

(800) 899-8454

www.wilsonlanguage.com

Printed in the U.S.A.

Step 4 Concepts

Vowel-Consonant-E Syllable

4.1 Vowel-consonant-e syllable in one-syllable words (**hope**, **cave**)

4.2 Vowel-consonant-e syllable combined with closed syllables (**combine**, **reptile**)

4.3 Multisyllabic words combining 2 syllable types (**compensate**, **illustrate**)

4.4 ive exception: no word ends in **v** (**olive**, **pensive**)

lime	ape	home
ride	cube	whine
lane	wide	cake
line	pole	flake
name	nine	vase

tube	plate	chase
white	rope	grade
state	vote	time
bike	mile	came
bone	cone	wife

smile	note	choke
dime	drive	safe
mine	flute	tape
share	joke	chose
wave	hide	hose

pile	close	bite
hope	wine	slope
these	plane	poke
rule	those	rise
scrape	throne	spoke

lake	prize	dare
skate	cave	dive
snake	shine	hole
cane	quake	tune
slide	trade	fire
whale	prune	spine
bake	like	grape
ripe	globe	mule
scare	wipe	case
tide	sale	care

shake	stone	save
maze	shave	bride
take	strike	base
file	brave	shape
Dave	Steve	Mike

Kate	Jane	Pete
Jake	Duke	James
June	safe	broke
hate	five	game
life	rake	late

+s

plates	ropes	games
stripes	whales	rules
rakes	globes	mazes
slides	likes	jokes
grades	votes	tides

+s

whines	flames	cares
bones	cases	shares
scrapes	hides	planes
waves	trades	dives
slopes	grapes	prunes

hope	cap	pin
cape	mop	bite
cut	hop	pine
not	mane	shin
hide	note	hid

cute	can	bit
mope	man	dime
tap	slide	pet
Tim	tape	slid
Pete	time	dim

quite	date	hire
code	daze	fake
hate	rude	slave
zone	prone	blaze
robe	scale	crave

drape	scrape	sane
mole	fade	stole
mute	sake	drone
dupe	glaze	grope
glare	pane	slate

stare	pride	shame
quote	haze	spade
chime	craze	dine
stale	clothe	stake
snipe	spike	thrive

rote	spare	swipe
flake	tote	gripe
scare	blare	yoke
flare	tone	bathe
blade	Blake	braze

stride	lobe	rite
lame	strobe	spite
dare	chafe	brute
lathe	trite	crude
hare	prune	fare

tithe	mole	rare
fife	bare	mime
cove	gale	spire
eke	dose	chive
lone	theme	nude

jive	yoke	twine
dune	rove	vane
cure	brine	mate
pure	hone	jade
mope	rave	pike

blame	tribe	spade
rife	drone	rate
spike	rate	probe
shrine	doze	slate
while	lame	slime

strikes	snores	hopes
flakes	gropes	states
zones	dines	strokes
hides	quakes	stores
panes	sites	codes

+s

dupes	chokes	fakes
rites	craves	scales
dives	times	hates
hires	gripes	scones
pokes	glares	trades

slope	plume	fad
vane	stripe	sham
rot	shame	bath
gripe	plum	grip
spite	cod	spit

node	slop	clothe
site	con	sit
cone	van	rote
fade	nod	code
strip	bathe	cloth

vime	quipe	jire
bode	draze	frope
gake	nole	blate
fline	grude	wose
slive	bine	flome

jope	smule	hape
prane	fote	glute
blate	chope	kine
dreve	scobe	dafe
scole	wime	creve

Nonsense Words

+s

stopes	mipes	priles
flubes	shebes	thrades
chotes	frines	snifes
tefes	vopes	drutes
ploves	scrobes	smotes

+s

hefes	sheves	stipes
whokes	prumes	clipes
zepes	quokes	blires
flimes	sipes	trutes
crutes	wames	thomes

frot | *frote*

spive	stin	frot
stot	spad	frote
thrap	prete	zin
shike	blire	quil
thepe	chim	quile

frot | *frote*

drene	smip	steke
dren	spale	shope
swite	quate	drim
clem	fush	slep
woth	fushe	triz

1   I like the tune that Kate will sing.

2   I left the bone on my plate.

3   Is it safe to ride my bike on that path?

4   I will trade this packet of gum.

5   The wise king sat on his throne.

6   I hope I get the best grade in math class.

7   Jane and Dave had a tennis game.

8   I think there is a snake in that hole.

9   Did Kevin and Ed admit that they broke the rules?

10   Dave will be quite late for the dentist at nine.

1   In the big mall, Kate got lost in the maze of stores.

2   I hope the packet of gum is in my jacket pocket.

3   Dad told a joke that made us all smile.

4   The tickets for the basketball game are on sale.

5   If you drive past the tunnel, you will miss the traffic.

6   Sid has a flute to bring to band class.

7   Beth got pink and white pants on sale at the shop.

8   Hank has a limp and must use a cane.

9   Did the tot choke on that nut?

10   The dentist told Mrs. Smith that she had the best smile.

1 Dad will drive the kids to tennis class and then go home and take a nap.

2 Let's slide down the slope and then go skate.

3 James will take the flag down off the pole.

4 That humpback whale was big!

5 Mike invented a game with lots of rules.

6 Find your helmet and then you can ride your bike.

7 Calvin is finishing the math quiz in time for lunch.

8 I will ride my fine bike.

9 We can go to the cave next to the lake.

10 The bride will have a fine time at her wedding.

1 Jane will save to get that dress.

2 The sun will shine on the pond.

3 If you win the game, you will get a prize.

4 Do not choke the pup when you hug him.

5 After we skate, we will go home.

6 James dove into the cold pond, but Hal and Jane did not.

7 We can slide on that hill slope.

8 That sudden blast made us all jump.

9 The plane will cross the Atlantic.

10 We will shake and bake the chicken.

1   We will make a cake with frosting and gumdrops.

2   I like it when the sun shines in the den.

3   The rules in this class are quite strict.

4   The plum is ripe but the grapes are bad.

5   I like to stroke my cat.

6   My dad has to shave and dress for the banquet.

7   Steve will tape his leg for the slam-dunk contest.

8   In June, we can swim in the lake.

9   Did Mom ask me to shake the rug?

10   Dad likes to save all this old junk.

1 Did Steve drop chestnuts in that hole?

2 Wipe up the mess and get the plates for lunch.

3 Kate will get the shrimp on sale.

4 It will take a long time to wipe up this mess.

5 Dave likes to scare the kids with his mask.

6 Spike, the cat, had a plate of fish.

7 The sun shines on that cactus plant.

8 Mike got the prize at the end of the contest.

9 Dave cuts the grass and then Alfred rakes.

10 Kenneth slid into home plate to win.

1 James did not have a spare when his tire went flat!

2 I hope to make a trade-in for this old van.

3 Pete fell off the rise of the big wave.

4 This ham sandwich is stale.

5 Dale insisted that we sit in the shade.

6 The stale smoke in the club made me ill.

7 We will share the bid to close the contract.

8 Jane extended her credit to get the red linen dress on sale.

9 Kate ate Dad's cake with pride.

10 The grandslam left the fans at the game in a daze.

1   Did Jake think that it was rude to stare?

2   Mrs. Tate had to grope for her cane to get out of the fire.

3   Kevin likes to dare his pal, Ed, to jump.

4   Mr. Jones held a ten of spades that was trump.

5   Steve Cole has a snapshot of a white whale.

6   Bill intends to shave and dress for the banquet at six p.m.

7   Glen was content to put on his robe and sit by the fire.

8   I suspect that the shop will close at nine.

9   Pete intended to get a spare tire for his van.

10   Mr. Jones must hire a consultant to get him out of the mess.

1 It is a shame that Kate lost her handbag when she was at the mall.

2 Pete hopes to impress Jan on their date.

3 James was quite glad that his stock investment was safe.

4 Ed will stoke up the fire and get us a hot drink.

5 Ted's handstand made me smile when I was sad.

6 The man will shake my hand if I grant his wish.

7 The instant Pete drove into the pole, he had whiplash.

8 I plan to attend the basketball game, but I will be late.

9 It is a shame that Mr. Lang went bankrupt.

10 In spite of the cold, Kendall will jog on the path.

1   Jane is singing a classic tune.

2   I like the jazz of Duke Ellington.

3   That rude comment made me upset.

4   I hope to hire Bob Swift, since he is the best man for the job.

5   I like to gaze at the sunsets in Texas.

6   I crave hot chicken salad for lunch.

7   It's such a shame that our mascot will miss the big game.

8   We will dine at home this eve.

9   The freshman class did not like the strict rules.

10   I do not wish to travel to the cold zone in that state.

1   Mrs. Ross has lots of pride in her children.

2   Pete is brave to enlist in the army.

3   Can you tell me the name of that dude with the rude kid?

4   The tame mule will take our bags up the cliff.

5   Yes, Jane would like a lime in her drink.

6   Kate did not wish to step up on the scale.

7   Mr. Jones will rise at seven a.m. and get the bus at nine.

8   Beth likes to quote the gossip from the shop.

9   When Jim ended his trip, he did not have a dime left to his name.

10   When they publish the profits, I hope that my stock shares will rise.

1   The columnist got a quote from Calvin.

2   Steve hopes that his stress lessens.

3   Willis had the stakes for the tent in his van.

4   Pat saves all his cash, but Ellen spends all of her profits.

5   The flames of the fire rose and extended up the wall.

6   James will not share his bad jokes with us.

7   Dave cuts the grass and then Dale rakes.

8   Justin likes his distinct role at the bank.

9   Ed snores in bed, but he does not think so.

10   The boss states that we must have a more consistent staff.

Fun with Dad

Dad likes to have fun with his children, Ben and Josh. They are just tots. The kids hide on Dad and he has to find them and chase them.

This game was lots of fun, but the kids did not tire and Dad did. Then Dad wore a mask and hid. Josh and Ben could not find him. At last, he sprang out to scare them, and they went running to Mom. Dad had to take off the mask so they could see it was fake.

The Cactus Plant

Mom had lots of plants in her home. Most of them did thrive. Then Jim hid the cactus plant in the drapes for a prank. Mom did not miss it.

Jim did not think of the plant and it was still hidden in the drapes. It felt the neglect. The sun did not shine in that spot. It was in the shade and there was a cold draft.

At last Mom saw the cactus plant. There was not much life left to it and she was quite upset! It was just a prank. The neglect had been unintended, but still, Mom was mad.

Was there hope for the plant? Mom gave it a sunbath and it came back to life. The cactus was up-lifted and Mom was glad at last.

A Fine Time on the Slope

Stan and Kate like to slide on the hill. It was a fine day to slide with lots of snow on the hill. Stan and Kate got the sleds in the shed. The sun gave the hill a fine shine. The slope was quite big!

Stan and Kate had the sleds at the top of the slope. The sleds went at a fast rate and it was fun. Stan's pet dog ran down the hill after the sleds. Then they had to drag the sleds back up to the top of the slope.

The next time Stan and Kate went down the hill, Stan had a spill! He went into a big snow drift. The crash did not make him stop. He had to brush off the snow, but he strode back up the hill to glide again.

It was late and the sun did fade. They made one last run down the big hill. It was now quite cold on the slope. Stan and Kate had to go home.

At last they got out of the cold. The fire in the stove was splendid! They had a hot drink and some cake. The day on the slope had been lots of fun.

Hank

Hank sat at home. He did not wish to dine by himself, but his wife, Kate, was on a trip. It would be a shame to have an old ham sandwich by himself. It had been a long week, and he wanted to go out.

Hank made a call to Ted, but Ted had plans. In spite of this, Hank went to the Shrimp Shed. He did not like to dine out by himself, but he did not wish to sit at home.

At the Shrimp Shed, Hank met Steve and Beth. He had not seen them for a long time. Steve asked Hank to sit and dine and Hank was quite glad. Hank made a date with them to get together with Kate when she came back home.

The Wire Contract

Jane and Tom had to fix the wires in their old cabin by the lake. They had to hire someone to do the job. Tom had the name of one man, but he was quite rude. Jane and Tom had time to spare. They collected bids for the contract.

At last, they got five quotes. The rude man had given the best quote. Dare they take the risk? Tom and Jane did not wish to save cash yet end up with a mess. They gave the contract to the man with the second best quote. He did a fine job.

The Quake State

In the west, the State of California is prone to quakes. Yet, in spite of this, people dwell there. In the past, quakes have hit many times. Not much can help combat this problem. A quake does not last long, but it is no joke. It can shake things up for miles. The state can be tranquil, and the jolt of a quake can come with a sudden thrust.

People in this zone expect it to happen again. They do not know when it will strike. They can only hope that the impact will not take homes or victims.

invite	campfire	mistake
flagpole	escape	bedtime
rosebud	handshake	kingsize
drive-in	close-up	classmate
baseball	springtime	milkshake

clambake	sunstroke	gatepost
grapevine	trade-in	state-wide
caveman	fishplate	inside
lifetime	drugstore	fishline
firemen	manhole	sunrise

admire	dictate	unsafe
pollute	trombone	volume
lineup	bedtime	inhale
costume	basement	lifelong
frustrate	fireball	takeoff
confuse	dislike	concrete
exhale	postpone	pavement
umpire	make-up	entire
software	vampire	stampede
collide	advise	compete

inflate	homemade	athlete
explode	include	clothespin
tadpole	complete	reptile
pancake	whalebone	spareribs
wildlife	frostbite	cupcake
handmade	landslide	salesman
pinhole	baseline	childlike
ringside	stovepipe	compare
clockwise	homesick	hemline
hotcake	statement	bagpipe

online	nameplate	cashmere
flashcube	upgrade	franchise
bobwhite	spitfire	wineglass
sidestep	backstroke	filtrate
fireside	crossfire	namesake

sidewise	windpipe	snaredrum
spokesman	sidetrack	crossbones
homeland	whitecap	landscape
made-up	grindstone	whitewall
postdate	flagstone	firetrap

nosedive	ragtime	telltale
limestone	sidelong	update
fanfare	primrose	wildfire
millstone	sideswipe	offside
farewell	shipshape	sulfate

makeshift	pipestem	wineskin
self-made	sunbathe	pileup
off-white	stoneware	slantwise
firebox	life-line	ninepins
oldline	mundane	all-time

exclude	inflame	compose
estate	aspire	impure
connive	oppose	pulsate
decade	expose	immune
hostile	impale	ignite

subside	lactose	encase
capsize	diffuse	gangrene
mandate	accuse	octane
translate	methane	intrude
midwife	condone	transpire

cascade	shipmate	convene
insane	fixate	invoke
incline	console	disrobe
flatware	inmate	commute
subscribe	filtrate	welfare

bonfire	enclose	yuletide
engrave	extreme	unclothe
inquire	confide	contrive
obscure	upscale	inscribe
transpose	membrane	ingrate

contrite	compile	excrete
connive	dispute	enthrone
adhere	impede	lignite
exude	concave	magnate
obtuse	disclose	baptize

despise	alcove	diffuse
encode	oxide	encode
uptake	tinware	firebug
milestone	sideslip	brimstone
impale	lactate	instate

capsate	inbefe	vilmite
trenzime	dispote	maseplod
transdope	exbale	vennape
conbrile	endame	filkipe
explobe	drenzime	plobbile

disfume	doselit	plebmat
poltrum	glibmax	fretjome
immone	laxtile	oppreve
drenvile	mentrabe	colgrone
pulvene	lebetrom	rettume

1   Mr. Wilkonson went inside the damp cave.

2   Dave will get a trombone in June.

3   Eve has a strong handshake!

4   It is unsafe to cross that lane of traffic.

5   The class reptile is lost in the lab.

6   Kate will complete the job the best that she can.

7   The red rug is in the basement.

8   I think that it was a mistake to ignore him.

9   Ben must take time to go vote for his classmates.

10   It's fun to sit by the campfire and sing songs.

1 My classmate got the top prize.

2 I think I will invite Zeke to the wedding.

3 I like the springtime best.

4 My milk and cupcake did not last long.

5 Jim is quite tall so he got a king-size bed.

6 I think that the kids plan to go to the drive-in.

7 This problem does frustrate me!

8 Steve and Tom sat by the fireside while Beth and Jan went out on the pond to skate.

9 The children were upset when it was bedtime.

10 Ed went to the Shrimp Shed and had a clam plate and a milk shake.

1   I bet that the class will dislike this math problem.

2   Steve had spareribs and french fries.

3   That software will cost us lots of cash.

4   Dad gave Jim a fine handshake.

5   Eve got a big base hit in the sandlot baseball game.

6   If we can win this baseball game, then we will go to the state-wide contest.

7   Dave Smith will be the umpire for the second game.

8   Tom drank a big milk shake, but Jane just had a Coke.

9   I hope that we can escape from this damp cave.

10   Let's have a cupcake and some milk.

1   Did you drop this mitten on the pavement?

2   I think that Jane is a fine athlete.

3   Pete and Jake will compete in the contest.

4   I do not like to make a mistake.

5   It is bad for your lungs to inhale the smoke.

6   The wire is in the basement.

7   Did you dislike that joke?

8   We must drive to the shop to rent a costume.

9   Dave will inflate the raft and then we can take it out on the lake.

10   Ed had pancakes and ham at brunch.

1 Can you compute those math problems?

2 Jan Russel will oppose that bill in Congress.

3 The volume of sales went up!

4 Ben will object to that entire plan.

5 I think that Kenneth will invite Jane to the prom.

6 Let's rent that vampire film for the kids.

7 The consultant will advise the staff.

8 Frank's old shed is such a firetrap.

9 The console TV will fit in this spot in the den

10 I like these off-white walls.

1 Dave fell on the flagstone and had to go to the clinic.

2 The boss gave a mandate to her staff.

3 I will inquire about the baseball game.

4 Use the best octane gas when you fill the tank in my truck.

5 Fred is the state's all-time best in basketball.

6 The infant can not have the lactose in milk.

7 Kendall recommended that we dispose of the old stove.

8 I hate this extreme cold!

9 Mr. Jones did have a dispute with the umpire during the entire game.

10 Jim is immune to his critics' insults.

1 We must compare this prospect with the other investments.

2 Did the wind subside at last?

3 Ignite a flame for the stove.

4 We must get an update from James.

5 Kate made a big mistake to sit under the sunlamp.

6 Milton had to wave farewell to Jane as she got on the nonstop jet to Manhattan.

7 The staff had to compile the list of old investments.

8 Mr. Chase did express thanks for his staff in his statement to the press.

9 Ethel put on makeup and lipstick.

10 The landscape here is fantastic!

1   We made a big bonfire for the clambake.

2   Ben had whitewall tires on his red Mustang.

3   Mr. Jiminez intended to sit at ringside.

4   The contract dispute ended at last.

5   The gong in the camp rang at sunrise.

6   The old man in this snapshot is your namesake.

7   Steve and Jim had a useless conflict about the job.

8   That ragtime tune made me smile.

9   I suppose it was a mistake to get that software.

10   Mike will pin up the hemline on those pants.

1 The men intend to invade the tribe.

2 Dad will not let those kids intrude on the game.

3 Did the stove explode to make such a blast?

4 It is a shame that you did not invite Steve and Kate.

5 The van fell into the pothole and got a flat tire.

6 We will get more concrete to finish the job.

7 I bet the congressman will win the vote by a landslide.

8 I can confide in my wife when I have a problem.

9 Did that van sideswipe my Mustang?

10 Do not let Dave impale the fish.

Complex Math

Tom did not finish his math problems. He intended to do them before math class, but he could not get them. He was upset. At lunch, he went to Mr. Jones, the math teacher. "I have spent a long time on this and I admit that I still cannot get the math," said Tom. "I can subtract, but I cannot get the entire problem."

"Well," said Mr. Jones, "these problems are complex. Jim can help you. He is the best at this. I suspect that lots of kids need help. I intend to do the problems step by step in class."

"Thanks," said Tom. "I will ask Jim to help me after I have lunch."

"You will still get credit for it, Tom," said Mr. Jones. "I am glad that you can ask for help when you cannot get the problems. I will see you in class."

In class, Mr. Jones said, "This math is complex! I suspect that many of you had a problem with it."

"Yes!" said Sanchez and Jake. "Most of the class did not finish."

"Well, do not panic. I will do the problems step by step," said Mr. Jones and he gave Tom a wink.

The Limestone Cave

Steve and Bev ran to get Gabe to explore a cave. Gabe felt that it would be fun to explore the limestone cave. Bev, Steve and Gabe made plans in the basement of Bev's home.

"Is the cave safe?" asked Steve.

"I think it is. I hope it is!" said Gabe.

"Let's take rope, just in case," said Bev.

The next day, they went to the cave. Inside the limestone cave, the rocks were damp. The sun did not shine in the cave. Gabe had a flashlight.

"I am brave," said Bev. "Let's go in."

Steve had his hand on the side of the cave. His hand felt something lifelike.

"Shine the flashlight here!" he said.

"What is it?" asked Bev. "Let me see."

"I think it's a bat!" said Steve.

"A bat! That is a bat! Let's go!"

Gabe, Bev and Steve left the cave fast. They ran to the lake and fell on the grass. "We were not so brave," said Steve. "I dislike a cave with bats!"

The Big Upset

Ed and Tim had a basketball game against the Tomcats. They had to rush; there was a strict rule about lateness. Mr. Duke, the coach, would explode if they were late. Ed was late; he had to tape his leg to compete or he would come up lame. Mr. Duke still let Ed in the game.

The fans were rude to the Tomcats. They wanted them to choke. It was a big game. Ed strode to the line to take the tip. He was not as tall in size, but he was an athlete and he could jump. Ed hit the ball to Tim. Tim made a fine shot from the side that did ignite his team.

At the end of the contest, Ed made a pass to Tim. Then Tim went to the basket. He was hit as a Tomcat made a swipe at the ball. The ball went in and credit was given for the basket. Tim went to the line to take a free shot. The Tomcats had made a big mistake. Tim's shot could win the contest and the time on the clock was about to expire. He did not panic and the shot went in! Ed did admire him. There was a stampede of fans.

Tim was splendid in the entire contest. Ed's game did not compare, but they did combine skills with the rest of the team to get the upset!

Pothole Problems

Flag St. had a big pothole in the concrete and this was a problem for travel. To drive to the West Campus, you had to go on Flag St. Still, the hole went neglected. Then a bus fell in the hole and got a flat tire. This held up traffic for some time, which made people quite upset. It had been a mistake to ignore the problem. Now there was a traffic mess to contend with. The next day, the hole was filled with gravel, and the pavement was fine again.

A

administrate	postponement	recognize
bare-handed	distribute	tranquilize
valentine	infantile	incomplete
custom-made	contribute	demonstrate
illustrate	infiltrate	contemplate

B

assassinate	immolate	disenfranchise
inundate	monoxide	atomize
safe-conduct	enfranchise	compensate
salesmanship	gamesmanship	victimize
confiscate	Chippendale	indispose

1   The vet must tranquilize the pup with a shot.

2   James must demonstrate his mistake on the math problem.

3   Kate was upset about the postponement of the game.

4   The costume is still incomplete.

5   That bobsled is second-rate.

6   We will contribute to the class fund.

7   Pete would like to get the custom-made chest for Kate.

8   Jake will help distribute the notes to the class.

9   Can you demonstrate that handshake again?

10 I think that Steve gave Robin a big valentine.

1   I like that Chippendale desk.

2   The cops will confiscate that cash.

3   Mr. Jones will hire Sheldon to administrate the West Campus.

4   Steve was closefisted when James made that rude comment.

5   We must find a talented consultant to illustrate the script.

6   The congressman's plans for this district are still incomplete.

7   Jake got the K.O. with a bare-handed punch.

8   His infantile statement did not escape the press.

9   I would like to contribute to Mrs. Smith's bid for Congress.

10   We did not recognize the truck after the crash.

1   That monoxide gas made me sick.

2   Mr. Jones will get advisement for the problem he will address soon.

3   When the boss got back from lunch, the job was still incomplete.

4   Patrick's stunt was infantile.

5   We must find a way to compensate for this loss in cash.

6   To end the seventh inning, Bill had to grab the pop-up bare-handed.

7   Ken will contemplate that problem.

8   Mr. Yang will distribute the tests.

9   All those votes will inundate the ballot box.

10 Mrs. Sanchez plans to compensate her staff well.

Valentine for Kate

Bob went on six dates with Kate. He did like her more than the other girls. It was then time to send a valentine. He felt like giving Kate the best valentine yet. He sat to contemplate this.

Bob was talented. He could illustrate quite well. At last he came up with a draft. He made it red and white. It was incomplete, but Bob still had time to finish it.

Bob felt he could make a statement to Kate with this valentine. The kind he could get at a drugstore did not compare! When it was complete, Bob did admire it. This valentine would make Kate glad.

Jane's Pup is Hit

Jane's pup, Spot, was hit by a van on Pride St. Jane had to call her mom to make a postponement of a shopping trip. Then she had to fix a custom-made sling. She felt so sad for the pup and did her best to console him.

Jane went to the pet clinic with Spot in the sling. The vet had to tranquilize him. Jane was restless. At last the vet came out with Spot. The pup did recognize Jane. Jane felt glad when she saw Spot wag his tail.

give	live	olive
active	massive	captive
disruptive	attentive	impulsive
expensive	impressive	inactive
expressive	inexpensive	inattentive

B

affective	inflective	compulsive
intensive	obsessive	connective
passive	subjective	constructive
expansive	inductive	distinctive
effective	extensive	submissive

1   The tot was active on the plane.

2   We live in Texas and Gabe lives in Boston.

3   That shrimp salad sandwich is expensive.

4   Mr. Stone will give his wife a big hug.

5   Cliff did not like the black olive.

6   For a joke, the kids held the pup captive.

7   Will we slide down that massive hill?

8   That kid in my class is quite disruptive.

9   Fred does act just a bit impulsive.

10   I hope that the red silk dress is inexpensive so I can get it for the banquet.

1   Steve did not think that Mr. Russel's comments were constructive.

2   The expansive land for sale in Wisconsin is a wise investment.

3   We cannot get that expensive console TV.

4   Congress must pass a bill to stop the sale of that addictive drug.

5   The script that Pete will publish is quite impressive.

6   For progress, we must invest in extensive software.

7   Ben will find a massive hill so he can slide.

8   Beth tends to be a bit compulsive when shopping at the mall.

9   I was inattentive to that long-winded statement.

10 Mr. Jones will get extensive help from Malcom.

1   It is so instinctive for my well-bred dog to hunt.

2   James lost the connective wire for the TV and VCR.

3   Yes, I do think that Gram's muffins are addictive!

4   Beth has the most distinctive smile in the entire class.

5   Kate will help us set the topmost objective for the club.

6   I do not think we can fix that massive problem.

7   That French king had an ineffective plan.

8   What is that offensive smell?

9   The bus trip to Kansas is quite expensive.

10   The intensive meeting lasted a long time.

The Not-So-Impressive Date

Jake made a date with Beth. She was rich and quite distinctive. He wanted to impress her. Jake got himself expensive pants and a top. He was then set for the big date.

Jake and Beth went to a banquet with Steve and Jan. Jake felt that Beth did like him. Then, all of a sudden, Jake was inattentive. This made him drop his plate of spareribs on his lap. His expensive pants were such a mess. This was not impressive! It made Steve, Jan and Beth poke fun at him.

In the end, Beth gave Jake a big kiss. She did like him with his mess and all! Jake was glad that Beth was not a snob and that she had fun.

Post Test Step 4

scrape	planes	illustrate
trombones	admire	expensive
postpone	springtime	dictate
valentine	clambake	umpire
olive	those	rosebud

constructive	demonstrate	whitecaps
craze	expose	compensates
compares	confiscate	suppose
impressive	probes	flatware
subscribe	victimize	sunbathe

Post Test Step 4

Nonsense Words

sheves	zake	fluse
glire	scrobes	exbale
vennape	drim	clipes
wames	plobbife	stathe
colgrone	trutes	immone

1 Circle any suffixes.

2 Scoop or underline syllables in basewords.

3 Mark syllable types, including exceptions.

4 Highlight **s** = /**z**/ in any vowel-consonant-e syllable.